SPREADGOOD

Copyright 2018

I'M KING OF THE JUNGLE. MY ROAR IS FAMOUS ALL AROUND THE WORLD
ROAR
ROAR
ROAR
ROAR

# ELEPHANT

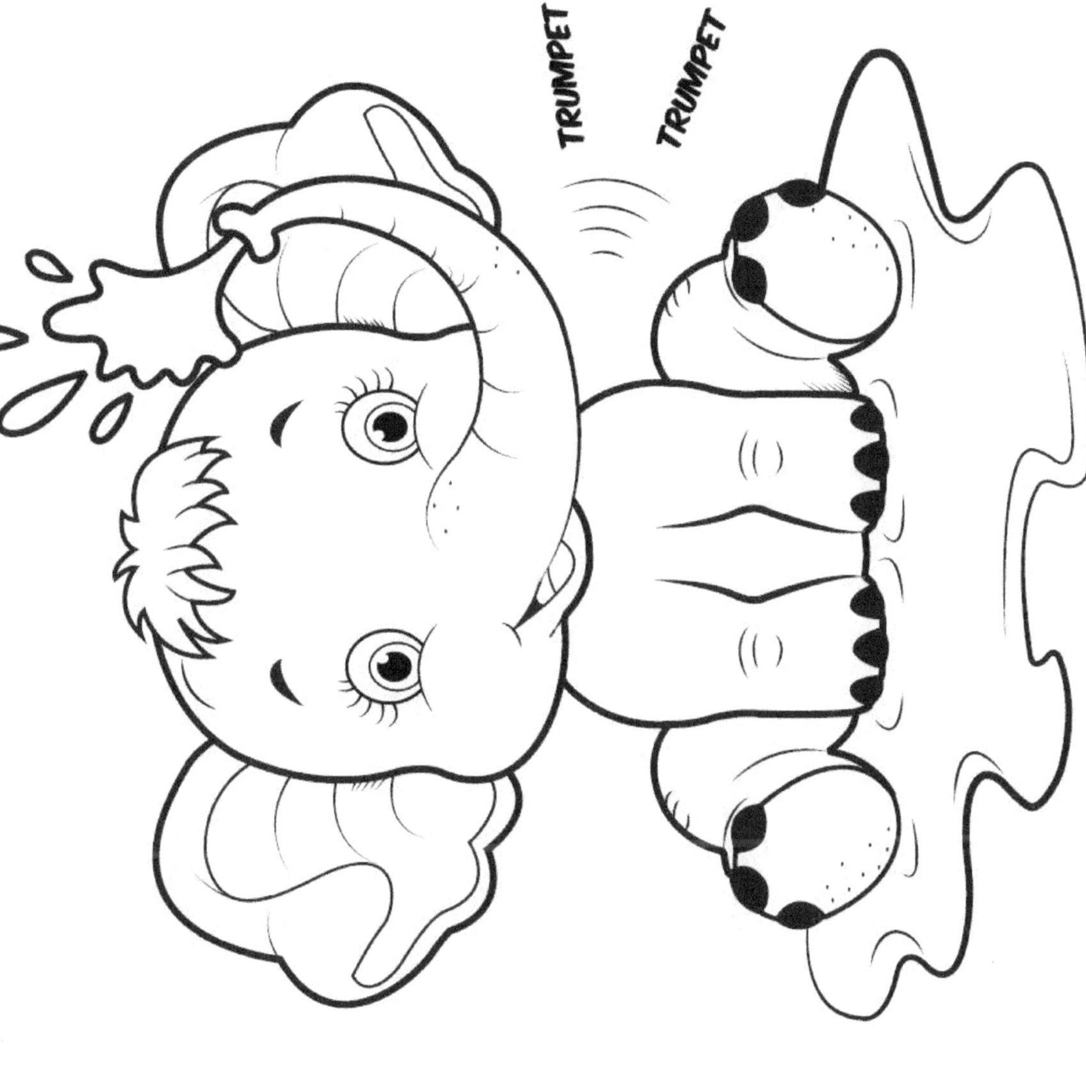

# COW

I AM KNOWN AS THE MOTHER AND
I GIVE MILK, IN THE HINDU SOCIETY
PEOPLE KEEP ME IN THEIR HOME.
MOO
MOO
MILK

# FOX

THE PHASE AS CUNNING AS FOX IS DERIVED FROM ME, AND THERE ARE 37 SPECIES OF FOXES LIVING IN THE WORLD.
BARK
BARK

PIG
I USE MY SNOUTS TO DIG, FOR ROOTS AND WORMS AS MY FOOD.OINK!!OINK!! 
OINK
OINK

# HORSE

I'M A STRONG ANIMAL KNOWN FOR RACING AND RIDING...NEIGH...NEIGH!!!!
NEIGH
NEIGH

GIRAFFE
I HAVE A REALLY LOOONGGGG NECK.
HUM
HUM

DEER

I HAVE AN EXTRAORDINARY SMELLING ABILITY. I CAN SMELL FOOD COMING FROM FAAAAAR....AWAY!!!
BLEAT
BLEAT

# POLAR BEER

MY BIG PAWS HELP ME TO WALK ON ICE AND SWIM IN THE SEA.
GROWL
GROWL

# RHINOCEROS

PANDA
I LIVE AROUND 20 YEARS IN THE WILD 
IN CHINA, AND MY DIET IS ENTIRELY
MADE UP OF BAMBOOO...
SQUEAK
SQUEAK
SQUEAK
SQUEAK

# KOALA BEAR

FOR THE FIRST SIX MONTHS, I AM SO CUTE I RIDE ON MY MUM'S BACK, USING HER POUCH TO FEED AND SLEEP.
GRUNT
GRUNT

I ALWAYS BECOME ACTIVE AT NIGHT AND SLEEP DURING THE DAY
OWL
HOO
WOO
WOO
HOO

I HAVE AN EXCELLENT EYESIGHT TO VIEW THINGS CLEARLY WHILE FLYING IN THE AIR...SCRE..SCREEE...!!!
EAGLE
SCRE
SCREEE

# PORCUPINE

A PORCUPINE HAS APPROXIMATELY 30,000 QUILLS ON ITS BODY THAT PROTECT AGAINST PREDATORS.
MOAN
MOAN

# HYENA

I'M WELL KNOWN FOR MY CACKLING LAUGH-LIKE SCREAM ....HEE...HEEE...HE!!!
HEE
HEE

PARROT

I AM KNOWN AS THE TALKING BIRD !!HELLOOO!!
SCREECH...SCREE
SCREECH...SCREE

BOAR
I ONLY COME OUT AT NIGHT TO FORAGE FOR FOOD...BLE...BLEE!!!
GRUNT
GRUNT

# LEOPARD

I'M A SUPER SPRING FAST FELINE AND RUN AT THE SPEED OF A 58KM/H!!!
YOWLS
YOWLS
YOWLS

# FROG

I CAN JUMP TO MY OWN HEIGHT
TWENTY TIMES.
!!CROC...CROCK..CRO!!
CROCK
CRO
CROCK

GORILLA
I EAT LOTS OF FOOD UP TO 29 KGS EVERY DAY, FROM WHICH I GET WATER TOO.
SCREAM
SCREAM

I CAN EAT AROUND 40 KG OF GRASS THAT'S WHY AM THE THIRD LARGEST ANIMAL IN THE WORLD.
HIPPOPOTAMUS
GROAN
GROAN
GROAN

ZEBRA
BECAUSE OF THE EXISTENCE OF BLACK
AND WHITE STRIPES ON MY BACK
I AM ONE OF THE MOST
UNIQUE SPECIES.
BRAY
BRAY
BRAY

I'M CONSIDERED TO BE ONE OF THE EARTH'S SMARTEST LAND SPECIES.
BARK
BARK
BARK
WOLF

CAMEL
I HAVE A LARGE HUMP ON MY BACK
WHERE I STORE FOOD AND WATER
EVERYONE CALLS ME
"THE SHIP OF DESERT"
GRUNT
GRUNT
GRUNT

# TIGER

I ROAR IN SUCH A LOUD SOUND THAM, THAT ANYONE CAN HEAR ME FROM 3KM AWAY...ROAR....ROA....!!!!
ROAR
ROAR
ROAR

I AM THE ANIMAL WHO DOES NOT LIKE TO BITE.
BARK
BARK
BARK
LLAMA

I AM A REPTILE,I AM HAVING ONE OF THE STRONGEST BITES IN THE WORLD.
CROCODILE
HISS
HISS
HISS

I SLEEP WHILE WINTER FOR 5 MONTHS, DURING WHICH I DON'T EAT AND DRINK. ...HUFF...HUFF..!!!
BEAR
HUFF
HUFF
HONEY

BECAUSE OF MY LOYALTY EVERYONE CALLS ME "MAN'S BEST FRIEND".
BARK
BARK

BAT
SCREECH
SCREECH
SCREECH
I'M THE ONLY MAMMAL WHO CAN FLY...

KANGAROO
I LIVE IN AUSTRALIA..I HAVE SPECIAL POUCH ON THE FRONT OF MY BODY FOR CARRYING A BABY.
GRUNT
GRUNT

REINDEER

I CAN LIVE IN A COLD, SNOWY CLIMATE.
DURING, CHRISTMAS TIME WE RIDE THE
SLEIGH TO GIVE PRESENTS TO CHILDERN
HO HO HO!!WINK!!!

BELLOW
BELLOW

IF I GET A SENSE OF DANGER,
I FREEZE WITHOUT MAKING A SOUND
SQUEAL...SQUE...!!!
MOUSE
SQUEAK
SQUEAK
SQUEAK

# GOAT

I AM ONE OF THE OLDEST DOMESTICATED SPECIES OF ANIMALS AND I GIVE MILK WHICH FORMS A SOFTER CURD. ....MAA...MAAA...MA...
MAA
MAA
MAA

I CAN RUN AT THE SPEED OF 55 KMS PER HOUR. I RUN ON TREES AS WELL AS ON POLES, WIRES, PIPES.
MONKEY
WHOOP
WHOOP
WHOOP

OX
I AM CONSIDERED TO BE ONE OF THE STRONGEST ANIMALS. THE PHASE AS STRONG AS AN OX IS DERIVED FROM ME.
BELLOW
BELLOW
BELLOW

SKUNK
I AM LEGENDARY ANIMAL KNOWN FOR MY BAD-SMELLING SPRAY...
SQUEAL
SQUEAL

# PENGUIN

I USE MY WINGS TO SWIM MORE FASTER UNDERWATER, INSTEAD OF USING THEM TO FLY IN THE AIR...
PEEP
PEEP
PEEP

TURKEY
I AM THE LARGEST BIRD ON THE FARM...
KEE-KEES
KEE-KEES
KEE-KEES

CHICK
I'M YELLOW IN COLOUR AND I
COME FROM THE HEN'S EGG
..PEEP.... PEEP...!!
PEEP
PEEP
PEEP

HEN
HUMANS KEEP ME AS A PETS AT THEIR HOMES, FOR BREEDING AND LAYING EGGS .
CLUCK
CLUCK
CLUCK

# DONKEY

I CAN CARRY LOADS WICH IS TWO TIMES MY BODY WEIGHT
HEE-HAW
HEE-HAW
HEE-HAW

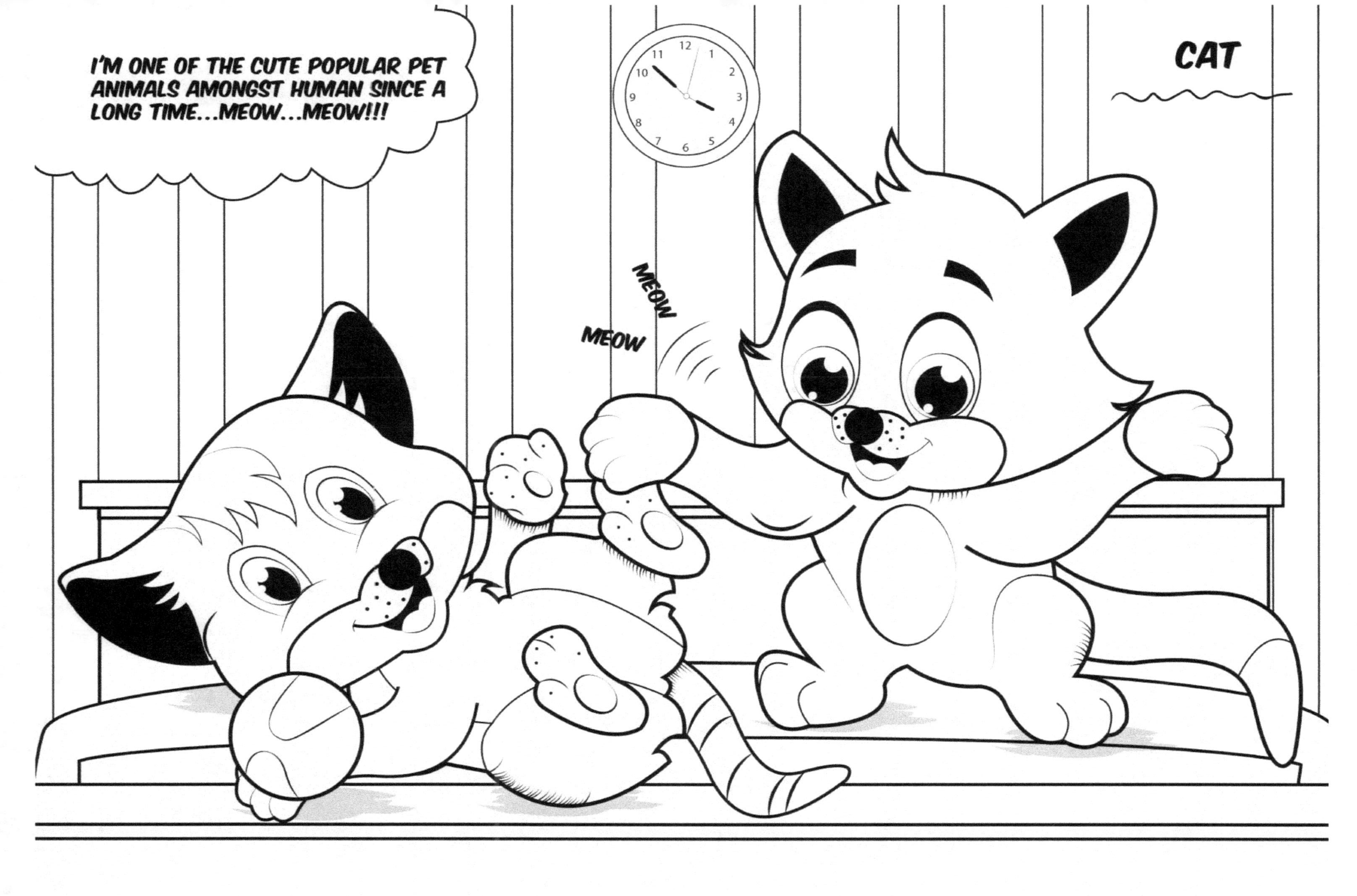

CAT
I'M ONE OF THE CUTE POPULAR PET ANIMALS AMONGST HUMAN SINCE A LONG TIME...MEOW...MEOW!!!
MEOW
MEOW

# PIGEON

I AM HIGHLY INTELLIGENT ANIMAL, I CAN FLY AT THE GREATER SPEED BECAUSE OF MY STRONG WINGS, AS FAST AS 70 TO 80 MILES PER HOUR.
COO-ROO
COO
COO-TOO

# WALRUS

I AM ONE OF THE LARGEST SEALS, SPENDING HALF OF THE TIME ON LAND AND THE OTHER HALF IN WATER.
KNOCKS
KNOCKS
KNOCKS

OTTER
I CONSUME BETWEEN 25 AND 40 PERCENT OF MY BODY WEIGHT DAILY TO KEEP MYSELF WARM. 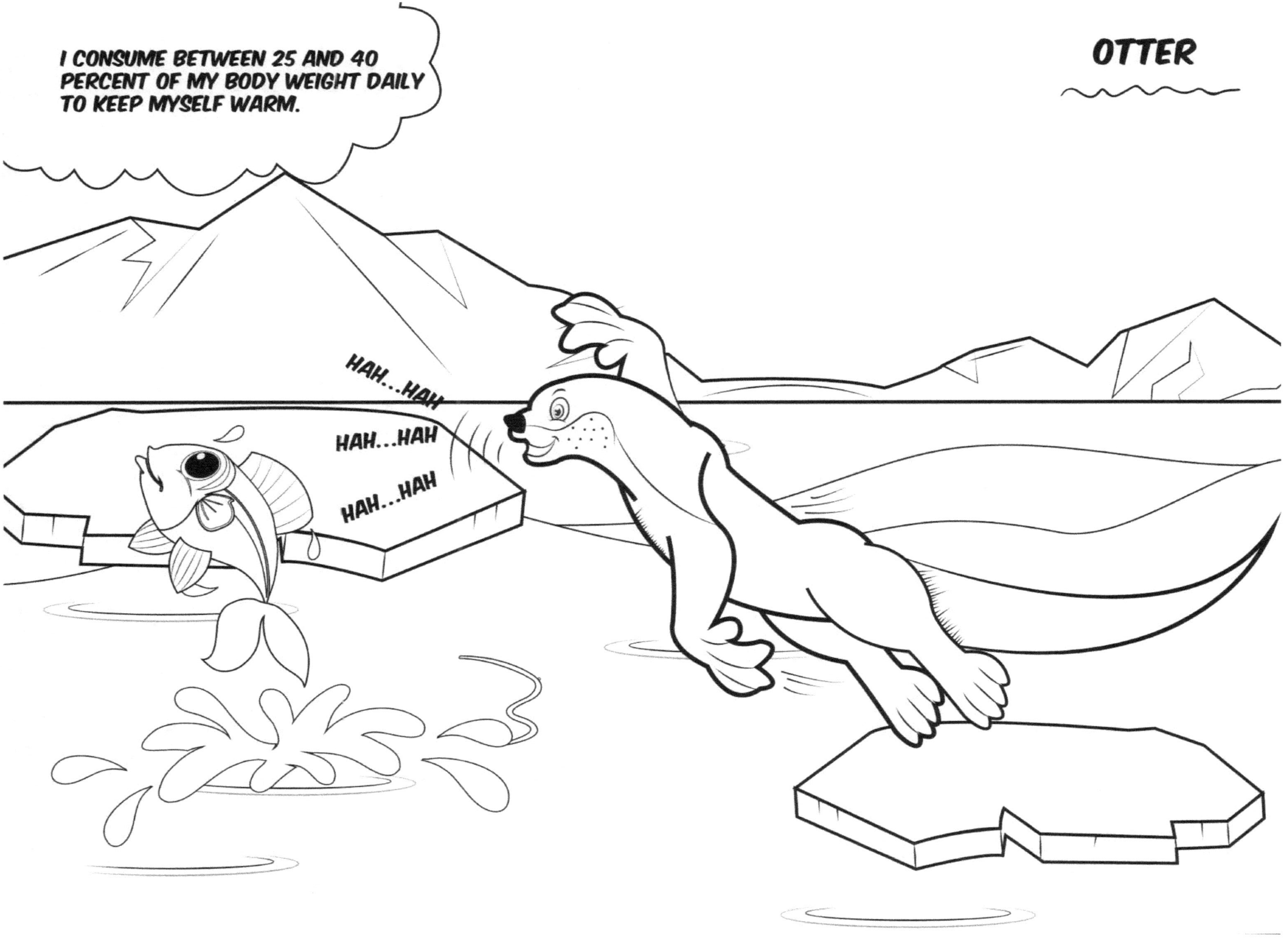
HAH...HAH
HAH...HAH
HAH...HAH

SEAL
I AM A HIGHLY INTELLIGENT MAMMAL.
I MIGRATE HUNDREDS OF MILES EVERY
YEAR IN SEARCH OF FOOD.
MOONS
MOONS

<u>**Thoughts from the publisher**</u>
Hi, we are spread good publications an independent publishing house that presents this book. The whole idea of the book is to spread the joy of coloring and explore the creative side of children. We hope you liked this book. Please do leave a review on amazon. We would highly appreciate it. We are small publication with a goal of spreading some joy. Some reviews will definitely help us boost and make great products for future also will help in letting the customer know about the book. :)

We believe in creating great content. So, if you have ideas or thoughts where we can make this book a better experience for children. Please do share your feedback on contact.spreadgood@gmail.com

<u>**Support**</u>

These activities will help focus by creating colored pages using different techniques. The role of decision-making during the process of drawing will be explored and reinforced. These exercises can help people who favor simple coloring to approach drawing in ways they may not have thought of before.